HERMAN GORTER

POEMS
OF 1890

A SELECTION

HERMAN GORTER

POEMS
OF 1890

A SELECTION

TRANSLATED BY PAUL VINCENT

≜UCLPRESS

First published in 2015 by
UCL Press
University College London,
Gower Street,
London WC1E 6BT

Available to download free: www.ucl.ac.uk/ucl-press

A CIP catalogue record for this book is available
from The British Library

ISBN: 978-1-910634-05-9 (Hbk.)
ISBN: 978-1-910634-06-6 (Pbk.)
ISBN: 978-1-910634-12-7 (PDF)
ISBN: 978-1-910634-10-3 (epub)
ISBN: 978-1-910634-11-0 (mobi)
DOI: 10.14324/111.9781910634066

Frontispiece: Herman Gorter, c. 1890, by Willem Witsen

These translations are dedicated in gratitude to Professor Emeritus Peter King, who introduced me to the work of Gorter and his contemporaries at Cambridge many years ago. The late Enno Endt, formerly of Amsterdam University, the greatest authority on Gorter's poetry, and my fellow translators Renée Delhez-Van der Wateren, John Irons and Francis Jones made valuable comments on my versions. Remaining imperfections are my own responsibility.

INTRODUCTION

HERMAN GORTER (1864–1927)

If the name of Herman Gorter is still familiar to anyone outside the Low Countries, it is more likely to be as a revolutionary propagandist and an opponent of Lenin's strategy at the Third International in 1920,[1] than as the most gifted Dutch poet of his age. At home he tends to be pigeonholed as the author of the poem *Mei* (May, 1889), the anthem of the Generation of 1880, while his other, particularly his Socialist, verse is largely neglected.

ROOTS

Gorter's father Simon, a minister in the non-conformist Mennonite church, which advocated adult baptism, social involvement and pacifism, was himself a talented journalist and writer. His death from tuberculosis in 1881 left Herman and his brother and sister in the care of a devoted and dominant mother, who moved her family from the rural surroundings of Zaandam to Amsterdam. A Mennonite upbringing left its mark on Gorter's social commitment and his independence of mind, while in his teenage years he was greatly influenced by the rebellious genius Multatuli (ps. Eduard Douwes Dekker, 1820–1887), author of the great colonial novel *Max Havelaar* (1860). Both Gorter's emotional dependence on his mother, and his attachment to and subsequent detachment from a succession of mentor/father figures, from the composer Diepenbrock to the German Marxist Karl Kautsky, can perhaps be attributed in part to this early bereavement.

The Netherlands in which he grew up, having been a European backwater for more than two centuries, was at last beginning to stir economically and socially. Its transport network of roads and canals was improved, its cities, particularly Amsterdam, expanded rapidly and there was new investment in heavy industries like steel and shipbuilding. Buoyed up by its profitable colonies in the East, the Netherlands slowly became a more dynamic, outward-looking and forward-thinking place – an attitude that extended to culture.

1   H. Gorter, 'Offener Brief an den Genossen Lenin', *Kommunistische Arbeiter-Zeitung* (Berlin, August-September 1920).

The young Herman was the beneficiary of a major reform in Dutch secondary education introduced in 1864, attending a new-style high school, the Higher Civic School (Hoogere Burger School or HBS), which played a crucial role in educating many young writers and intellectuals. Ironically, though the syllabus at these schools was largely science and modern language-based, Gorter's great love was Classical studies, which he went on to study at Amsterdam University, where he was prominent in his student debating society and where in 1889 he received his doctorate for a thesis on Aeschylus' use of metaphor (after a more daring project on poetic inspiration was rejected). Shortly afterwards he was appointed to his first post as a Classics teacher in Amersfoort and the following year married his fiancée Wies Cnoop Koopmans, despite some last minute doubts. Those doubts were not unfounded. The couple remained together until his wife's death in 1916, but it was an 'open' marriage, at least on Gorter's side, and a childless one. The poet's powerful erotic drive sought an outlet in two intense long-term relationships, with Ada Prins and later with Jenne Clinge Doorenbos, of which he made no secret. Both inspired memorable love poetry and Jenne, herself a writer, became his editor and collaborator as well as his muse (whom he dubbed, in Nietzschean style, 'the Spirit of Music').[2]

POETIC DÉBUT

In the same year he published his first Dutch poetry in the influential magazine *De nieuwe gids* (The New Guide). The journal, founded in 1885, was dominated at this period by the poet Willem Kloos (1859–1938), who used its pages to proclaim a radical aestheticism and advocate literature that was both non-sectarian and non-utilitarian. Poetry, Kloos famously asserted, was 'the supremely individual expression of the supremely individual emotion'. Kloos was deeply impressed by Gorter's début, *Mei* (May, 1889), an epic poem of some 4,000 lines, mostly in rhyming five-foot iambics (not coincidentally the metre of Keats' 'Endymion'), which soon became an iconic work of the so-called Movement of 1880. (Puzzlingly, only fragments of this seminal poem have so far been translated into English.) Generations of Dutch secondary schoolchildren have been able to quote its opening lines:

---

2   A selection of Gorter's letters to both women has been published by Lieneke Frerichs under the title *Geheime geliefden*, Amsterdam, 2014.

A newborn springtime and a newborn sound:
I want this song like piping to resound
That oft I heard at summer eventide
In an old town, along the waterside –
The house was dark, but down the silent road
Dusk gathered and above the sky still glowed,
And a late golden, incandescent flame
Shone over gables through my window-frame.
A boy blew music like an organ pipe,
The sounds all trembled in the air as ripe
As new-grown cherries, when a springtime breeze
Begins its upward journey through the trees

A number of features are immediately apparent even from this short extract: vivid sensory images, a celebration of the Dutch landscape, Homeric-style extended similes, and the onward impulse of the lines with their frequent enjambements. In all senses the poem came as a breath of fresh air in a literary culture dominated by plodding moralistic verse, often churned out by clergymen-poets. *May*, however, is not all joyful celebration: an underlying melancholy increasingly asserts itself. The poem's heroine embodies the month of May and her burgeoning prime is destined to be short-lived. Her encounter with the blind Norse god Balder (for whom 'music is the soul's life') is a poignant dramatisation of the unbridgeable dichotomy between mind and body. It is scarcely surprising, in a country steeped in Biblical criticism and exegesis, that whole libraries should have been written on the interpretation of the poem's symbolism, endlessly debating whether the poem should be read as a variation on Nietzsche's *Birth of Tragedy from the Spirit of Music*, whether it conceals Gorter's incipient disaffection from the values of 1880, whether it portrays the incompatibility of the material and the spiritual, or on the contrary presents a synthesis between them, etc. In a letter, the poet himself played down the ambiguities, declaring that:

> I wanted to make something full of light and beautiful sound, that's all. There's a story running through it, and a bit of philosophy, but that's by accident, so to speak.[3]

3   To his uncle K. Gorter, 23 March 1889.

Perhaps Gorter is being rather disingenuous here. It is hard not to see the poem at least in part as an exercise in 'lyrical autobiography', while others have pointed to the presence of two opposing impulses throughout his work: lyrical compression and epic expansion. One of his earliest efforts was the ambitious 'Lucifer', partly inspired by his reading of Milton. Gorter's expansive mode, which is particularly apparent in his later even larger-scale Socialist poems, *A Little Epic* (1906) and *Pan* (1916), met with critical resistance. At the other extreme is the almost haiku-like compression of the late love poems, *Liedjes* (Songs), most of them published posthumously, which form a private lyrical counterpoint to his public political statements:

All things fade quite
When you dance into sight.

Maybe, though, the distinction should not be seen as an absolute one: 'lyrical expansiveness' in fact characterises some of the poet's best work, in this collection and elsewhere. As one of his sternest critics, Anton van Duinkerken, conceded, Gorter was 'great in jubilation'.

ICON OF A GENERATION

Given the warm reception of *Mei* by most of his peers and by younger, progressive readers, Gorter might have been expected to continue in this epic vein. Instead, under the influence of the critic and novelist Lodewijk van Deyssel (1864–1952), his next chosen guru, whose response to the poem was less than rapturous, the *Poems of 1890* mark a radical new departure, not only in a Dutch but in a European context. Van Deyssel had called for an uncompromising form of individualism, for which he coined the term 'sensitivism', the recording of fleeting, fragmentary moments of experience with an almost mystical intensity. Gorter's collection is, in part, an attempt to realise Van Deyssel's vision. The only obvious point of comparison for this new-found artistic and verbal extremism is the Rimbaud of 'Le bateau ivre', 'Voyelles' and 'Un saison en enfer' (two of which also use rhyme as a binding medium, while the third alternates prose and poetry), though there does not seem to be any direct influence.

The result was a series of a hundred or so poems, some of only two lines (for example, 'You're a dusky white lily girl, /You're a butterfly velvet swirl.') and none longer than a few pages, still retaining a thread of rhyme, mostly in full rhyming couplets. It needs to be stressed that unlike elsewhere and specifically in the Anglo-Saxon world, modernism in the Low Countries is not synonymous with blank or free verse (like that of Eliot or Yeats). Attachment to rhyme persists in such interwar poets as Nijhoff and after the Second World War in the remarkable work of Achterberg. Set against this are irregular line lengths and syntax, a radical use of neologism, synaesthesia, surging eroticism, a haunting fragmentary musicality and occasional astonishingly simple and direct love poems. Gorter's explosive and sometimes tortured expressionism recalls that of his contemporary Van Gogh. His linguistic extremism is one of the main challenges for the translator.[4] Gone is the vaguely Classical and Norse framework of *May*, which may have been the legacy of Gorter's close relationship with his fellow-student, the composer Alphons Diepenbrock (1862–1921), a keen Wagnerian. This is a celebration of life in a different key, but, as in *May*, beneath the energy and assertiveness there lurks a sense of alienation and even despair.

The contrast with the work of his first mentor Kloos could not be more striking. While Kloos' solipsism ('Deep in my inmost thoughts a god I tower') is contained in conventional forms like the sonnet and the mood is autumnal and elegiac, Gorter's energy is life-affirming – he was a keen sportsman and outdoor enthusiast – and 'his' season is unquestionably spring. The following poem evokes the parallel approach of spring and of the beloved:

> The spring comes from afar, I hear it come hither
> and the trees hear too, the tall trees that shiver,
> and the tall skies, the heavenly skies,
> the tingle-light skies, the blue-and-white skies,
> shiver skies.

4   The critic Edmund Gosse, whose background essay 'The Dutch Senstivists' prefaced both the English translation of Louis Couperus' novel *Noodlot* (*Footsteps of Fate*, 1891) and the US edition of Couperus' *Eline Vere* (1892), derived most of his information from the young writer Frederik van Eeden (1860–1932), very much a literary insider. However, Gosse made one spectacularly erroneous claim: '... the Dutch seem ... to leave their mother-tongue unassailed, and to be as intelligible as their inspiration allows them to be.' Even the most cursory reading of *Poems of 1890* would have corrected that misapprehension.

Oh I hear her come,
oh I feel her come
and I'm filled with fright
at trembling desires, all bright,
just about to break ...

But exaltation alternates with a perplexed alienation that can assume almost surreal form:

... Across the world's face
things were probably alike,
the world and the human race
are scarcely alive.

I walked and watched the scene
scared and content,
below, ever loyal and keen,
my footsteps bent.

CHANGING COURSE
The sense of a disintegrating world and an increasingly isolated self became so strong in Gorter that after publishing these poems he began, like a number of his contemporaries, to look inwards and seek a unifying philosophical framework. He found this briefly in Spinozan thought, which stressed the oneness of all being, possibly under the influence of his fellow-poet Albert Verwey (1865–1937), but still felt disconnected from the huge social and political struggles convulsing Europe at the time that were to culminate in the First World War and the Russian Revolution. A collection of 1895 (*School of Poetry II, 2*) ends with a cry of anguish:

Oh God! The side I'm standing on is wrong.
I'm going under.
My love has come to nought.

In 1897 he resolved to act and joined the fledgling Social Democratic Workers' party (SDAP) led by Pieter Jelles Troelstra (1860–1930), and his poetry now evoked the triumph of the revolution, sometimes in a naïve mode that drew mockery from his former literary allies:

> The working class dances a great round
> along the shore of the world's Ocean ...

His inspiration will henceforth be the glorious future rather than the elusive, vanishing present; where the bourgeois individual was isolated, the Socialist individual will be one with his fellow men. This optimism is typified by his dutiful celebration of the national railway strike of 30 January 1903:

> Something great has happened in this little land,
> Have you heard? The railwaymen have
> of their own free will supported
> the stevedores, not selfishly but for their mates.
> The fire of solidarity has spread
> – its flames stretch wider – all for one
> and one for all in the working class!

The above lines may be conversational, even prosaic, but in general Gorter's verse becomes noticeably more regular, often reverting to the sonnet form, and his imagery more conventional.

In 1909, tiring of the SDAP's constitutional gradualism, he left to form the splinter SDP party (the nucleus of the later Dutch Communist Party), encouraged and assisted by such allies as Karl Kautsky and Anton Pannekoek. In 1920, having travelled clandestinely to Moscow for the Third International, after an epic six-week journey, partly hidden in the hold of a ship repatriating Russian prisoners-of-war, he addressed a critical Open Letter to Lenin – in response to Lenin's own earlier scathing attack on 'Leftists' in his *Teething Troubles of Communism* (1920) – which argued for a different revolutionary approach in Western Europe from that taken in Russia (given, for example, the very different status of the peasantry), abandonment of the opportunistic use of existing parliamentary and union structures, a less dominant role for the peasants and an intelligentsia-led campaign of direct action. All this was perfectly consistent with his conviction that revolution must start 'from the bottom up'. Gorter's proposals were laughed out of court, especially by Trotsky.

Gorter's merits as a propagandist had been acknowledged by Lenin before their clash[5] and a steady stream of articles, pamphlets and books continued to flow from his pen, appearing at home and abroad in such publications as Sylvia Pankhurst's *The Workers' Dreadnought*, where he argued for the necessity of a Fourth Workers' International to oppose the centralism of Moscow (1921). His most influential work was undoubtedly his widely translated *Historical Materialism Explained for Workers* (1908). While conceding that truths are historically determined, this work reveals Gorter's belief in a core of dynamic individualism that was anathema to the Bolshevik leadership and an inspiration to free spirits in the Marxist movement. 'We do not make history of our own free will. But ... we do make it ... not through blind fate, but through living society.'

Interestingly, the book's greatest and most lasting impact may have been in China, where his committed translator, Li Da, used the German and Japanese translations to produce his version and wrote extensively to promote Gorter's reservations about economic determinism. One possible convert, direct or indirect, to the cause may have been the young Mao Zedong.[6] It is tempting to contemplate what Gorter would have made of post-Mao economic reforms and human rights abuses in China.

DISTANTIATION FROM THE MOVEMENT OF 1880

As a man of letters, Gorter disowned the individualism of his former allies in the *New Guide* group in his 'Critique of 1880' (1897–1900) and in a series of critical essays in *The Great Poets* (collected posthumously in 1935), he extolled figures like Aeschylus, Shakespeare and especially Shelley, who combined sensibility with revolutionary fervour. It is in this work that he gives his striking, if simplified, definition of the unconscious – he had dismissed Freud's explorations as a bourgeois distraction:

> The unconscious is not, as bourgeois writers believe, an unknowable, mysterious power. It is perfectly knowable, and consists of three forces: the urge to self-preservation or love of self, the sexual urge or love for woman, and the social urge or love for the community.

5   Letter of 5 May, 1915, Lenin, *Collected Works 43*, Moscow, 1977, pp. 453–454a.
6   N. Knight, 'Herman Gorter and the Origins of Marxism in China', *China Information* 2005, 19, 381–412.

ARE POETRY AND POLITICS COMPATIBLE?

His principal poetic work after his conversion to Marxism is the epic *Pan* (1912, rev. ed. 1916). In it Gorter unfolds a Utopian vision of a post-revolutionary world, generally playing down the necessary intervening violence and bloodshed, though the second expanded edition of 1916 does allude to the pointless slaughter of the international working class on the battlefields of the First World War:

> ... Choked in the gases, slaughtered by
> Bullets, torn asunder by mines
> The Workers lay strewn on the earth.
> Sacrificed by their rulers and omnipotent
> Capital, to bring them Possession
> Of the Earth the Workers lay
> Dead and dismembered all across the Earth.

The sincerity of Gorter's compassion, anger and sense of waste is patent, but compared to, say, the raw immediacy of a Wilfred Owen, these lines seem distant and generalised (the Netherlands was neutral in the conflict, and as a Socialist Gorter saw the war as a capitalist-orchestrated distraction from the rising tide of revolution).

Gorter was accused in some quarters of having quit literature for the simplifications of dialectical materialism, but he himself saw his work as a continuum. In his socialist poems we hear the voice of a benign revolutionary anxious to share his joy in the world with all classes. His epic *Pan* ends with a moving, renewed commitment to the art of poetry:

> From childhood on I felt you, poetry,
> I can remember nothing of which you weren't
> Part. The reflection of my thoughts,
> That I sensed in all things, was you.
> The sweet murmur of the sea, my Mother's voice,
> The gait of my comrades, the light
> Of the world. People walking. The night. [...]
> Love itself meant nothing but for your sake.
> The body's deepest joy meant nothing to me.
> Women's dark womb meant nothing to me.

The oblivious self-giving meant nothing,
Except that I found deep in their womb,
Deep in the infinite obscurity
Nothing but you – you, you, dear poetry.

Gorter was a formative influence on his contemporary Jan Hendrik Leopold (1865–1925), and on the post-Second World War generation of 1950s poets, especially Lucebert (ps. Lubertus Jacobus Swaanswijk, 1924–1994), who defiantly borrows the name of one of Gorter's collections, 'School of Poetry', for his own didactic 'little revolution' in literature. Gorter remains one of the greatest love poets in Dutch; it is no accident that in both his very first preserved poem and in the one he finished just before he died, love is central. Indeed, '*Liefde*/love' is the very last word he wrote as a poet, recalling the final line of the masterpiece of his beloved Dante.

In the last collection to be published in his lifetime, *Het ontbrokene* (The Lack, 1990), one of the Low Countries' pre-eminent late-twentieth-century poets, Hans Faverey (1933–1990) included 'Gorter on the Shore', an enigmatic picture of Gorter as tennis-player, Classicist and poet that evokes the solitude and the interweaving of nature and myth in the work of his great predecessor. Two extracts seem to me to provide a fitting epitaph:

As if he's standing there, there
where the beach is narrowest,
at the foot of his dune –
a perhaps already somewhat
tanned, obstinate man: like
someone looking out to sea,
but alone with himself ...

... It's Arrianus[7]
who describes Epictetus'

doctrine of the little
that one honourably possesses. Nonetheless,
whenever there's someone who hasn't forgotten

7   Arrianus was the editor of the Stoic Epictetus; Sheria is a kind of Utopia in the *Odyssey*. None of Faverey's allusions, Classical or political, would have been wasted on Gorter.

Scheria, and who continues to re-read some lines
of this unbending man, precisely this
vain amount, conquered from the bright sea
beach, cannot be erased by any more poetry.

GORTER IN TRANSLATION

The select bibliography of Gorter's poetry in translation shows that while
there has been some international exposure for his shorter lyrics and
fragments of *May*, most translators have shied away from his two great
epics, pre-Socialist and post-Socialist, in their entirety. This distorts not only
the picture of Gorter's poetry for those without Dutch, but also his position
within the Dutch canon.

As for English versions, these are mostly quantitatively and qualitatively
disappointing. Gorter's first English translator, A.L. Snell, makes an imaginative
choice for inclusion in his anthology *Flowers from a Foreign Garden* (1902). Sadly,
his rendering of the great poem 'De lente komt van ver/The spring comes from
afar' (see above) is stilted and occasionally inaccurate.

Adriaan Barnouw (1948) also tackles a poem from the present
collection, 'Mijn liefste was dood/My dearest had died', which gives
something of the flavour of the 'sensitivist' Gorter, but the excerpt from *May*
in his anthology *Coming After* captures neither the insistent rhyme nor the
compelling rhythm of the original.

By far the most substantial contribution thus far has been that of
Theodoor Weevers (1960). Weevers has a musician's ear for the cadences of
May, and also ventures beyond the poem's perhaps over-familiar opening,
including a long section from Book II on the crucial meeting of May and
Balder. He does justice to his choice from *Poems of 1890*, 'Een roode roos is
in mijn hand/A red rose is in my hand', produces a convincing version of a
sonnet from a transitional period, and finally with great sensitivity conveys
the mood of one of the best known and most triumphant statements of
Gorter's new-found happiness and sense of belonging after embracing the
Socialist cause:

The day is opening like a golden rose;
I'm at the window and my breath goes out,
the field is still, and hardly one lone sound
breaks toward the blue dome in this quiet pause.

And in my room like a dark box enclosed,
where pearls are hanging on the window-pane,
I'm walking up and down to where, hemmed in
by the dark wall, in deeper thought I pause.
I now have found it, mankind's happiness,
though I have lived through four and thirty years
before I found it, and oft failed in stress
of vain endeavour and in strife that wears.
But so surely as out there the sun has bound
the world in haze, that happiness I've found.

One may occasionally quibble with Weevers' conservative idiom and choice
of words, but his empathy with the source text is apparent at every turn. His
work testifies to a profound knowledge and love of both Dutch and English
poetry of the period, as befits an expert on the previously mentioned poet
Albert Verwey, of whom he was a pupil.

It is interesting in this context to compare Weevers' account of this
watershed poem with that of an eminent contemporary translator of Dutch
poetry, John Irons:

The day's unfolding like a golden rose;
I send my breath out at the window-sill,
there's scarcely any sound – the fields lie still –
that rises to the blue sky's vaulted dome.

And in my boxlike room, completely black,
in front of which the pearls hang on the pane,
I pace the floor until I'm stopped again
and quietly muse when dark walls halt my track.

I've found it, human happiness, despite
it taking four and thirty years for me
to do so, and much searching failed outright
through tussles, gestures made quite needlessly.
As sure though as the world outside is dressed
in veils of sunlight, I've found happiness.

Irons, who has had a number of attempts at translating the poem, comments: 'I remember reading this opening line for the first time in late-1962. At the time it seemed ample proof to me that the Dutch language could be beautiful – a view I have since always held.'

There is undoubtedly still much work for English Gorter translators to do. Of my own versions, the product of a number of years' intense confrontation with this collection, I will say only that I have tried to steer a middle course by retaining as much as possible of his frequent 'foreignness' in Dutch, avoiding overtranslation or overinterpretation, while not totally alienating English readers. Gorter's consistent use of rhyme, which has been mentioned previously, combined with his incantatory use of repetition, presents a challenge to the translator wishing to escape a 'jingle effect'. Wherever possible, I have tried to respect the original's periodic use of lighter, feminine rhyme (with an unstressed final syllable), but semantic and stylistic constraints have occasionally led to these being lost in translation.

An eminent authority on the poet, to whom I showed samples of my work, lamented the absence of the unique 'music' of the originals. Initially I was very crestfallen at this reaction, but then reflected that my critic had probably never read or heard Gorter in English translation and anyway that the music he had in mind was, by definition, untranslatable. I have sought not to reproduce that music, but to transpose it into a different idiom. How successful I have been, is for the reader to judge.

Paul Vincent

POEMS
OF
1890

Toen de tijden bladstil waren, lang geleen,
is ze geboren, in herfststilte een bloem,
die staat bleeklicht in 't vale lichtgeween, –
regenen doen de wolken om haar om.

Ze stond bleeklicht midden in somberheid,
de lichte oogen, 't blond haar daarom gespreid,
de witte handen, tranen op meen'gen tijd,
een licht arm meisje dat lichthonger lijdt.

Breng over haar bloemgloede kleuren, uw
bloedrood, o nieuwe getijde dat is nu.

When no leaf stirred, long ago in the past,
she was born, autumnal silence's bloom,
standing pale-bright while light weeps, overcast:
rain falls from the cloud banks that loom.

Amid the grimness she stood pale-bright,
her bright eyes by blond hair were circled tight,
tears often flowing, hands all white,
a poor light girl who's hungry for light.

Paint her with bloom-glow hues, with your
blood red, new age who're standing at the door.

Ik zat toen heel stil te werken,
de boeken waren als zerken
voor me, ik wist wel wat
elk graf in zich had.

Mijn lijf zat daar in een kamer,
boomtakken voor het raam er
heenkropen en weer vervelend,
met groene bladen al geelend.

Mijn oogen zagen verwonderd
naar 't buitenlicht, maar zonder 't
zelf te weten wat of
hun licht oppervlak trof.

O mijn hart was toen zoo hongerig,
zo angstig en zoo verlangerig,
zoo droog en het regende niet
en elke dag ging te niet.

Ik zat in die lichte dagen –
mijn hart hield nooit op te jagen –
ik zat te zien en te werken,
alles was me als doodzerken.

I once sat quietly and read,
the books like tombs for the dead
before me, I knew just what
was in each grave plot.

My body sat in a room inside,
tree branches crossed panes outside,
irked me and crept to and fro,
green leaves gained an ochre glow.

Amazed, I looked up to the skies
outside, but couldn't surmise
what it was or how
that struck their light surface now.

Oh, then how my poor heart hungered,
and so trembled and hankered,
so dry and it would not rain
and each day passed in vain.

I sat in those days of light –
my heart raced in endless flight –
I sat using my eyes and head
it all seemed like tombs for the dead.

O als de zon schijnt
en de aarde wegkwijnt
in dien luister
weg in 't duister,
en maar scheem'rend het hoofd
opheft in schauw omloofd –
treedt nader, treedt nader
blankvoeten te gader
te gader de voeten, de handen –
de lachtande
de blauwooge
de blond hooge
de zilverwoorden weenende,
het lijnig hoofd leenende
achterover omhoog in de lucht –
zoet, zoet, langzaam vlucht
door het zonnedagen
in de hooge hagen
zon – zoet zoet langzaam vlucht,
ga niet te gauw voorbij, voorbij, voorbij, de lucht
blijft hangende bevende achter u –
verlangende eeuwig naar u
eeuwig, eeuwig – vlucht niet te vlug –
achter uw rug
rek ik de armen
van verlangen, van verlangen
rek ik de armen,
vlucht niet te vlug.

Oh when the sun shines
and the earth fades and pines
in that lustre
where shadows cluster,
and its head dimly heaves
shrouded in shadowy leaves –
come hither, come hither
you white-feet together
together the hands, the feet –
laugh-toothed
blue-eyed
blond-high
silver-word keening one,
lined head-leaning one
backwards up to the sky –
sweet, sweet, slowly fly
through the sun's first glow
in the tall hedgerow
of sun – sweet sweet slowly goes by,
don't pass too soon, pass, pass, the sky
still hangs trembling behind you –
forever longing for you
forever, forever – don't fly too fast –
as you pass
I stretch out my arms
in longing, in longing
I stretch out my arms,
don't fly too fast.

O hoe blank zijt ge van rug,
zongebrand, uitgeglansd vleesch –
waar het tot schouder oprees,
waar de lichte haren
in trillende snaren
in de zonnescharen
hangen saam in de lucht,
in de lucht in de lucht
terwijl gij vlucht.

Als de zon schijnt
en de aarde wegkwijnt
wèg in het duister –
en dan wèg de luister,
uwe luister,
alle luister.

Your back is oh so white,
    tanned flesh no longer glows –
where to the shoulders it rose,
where light hair stands
in trembling strands
mid suns in vast bands,
merging on high,
up on high, up on high
as you fly.

Oh when the sun shines
and the earth fades and pines
where shadows cluster
and gone is the lustre,
your lustre,
all lustre.

Gij zijt een stille witte blinkesneeuw,
gij zijt een blinke zeeë tintelzee.

You're a silent white gleam of bright snow
You're a gleamy sea-filled tingle sea.

Gij zijt een schemerwitte leliemeid,
Gij zijt een wijde vlinderveluwheid.

You're a dusky white lily girl,
You're a butterfly velvet swirl.

Gij zijt het opene, het witte, 't willende,
Het wachtend, straalvlammend, lichtlillende.

You're the open one, white, and willing,
waiting, beam-blazing, light-trilling.

De zon. De wereld is goud en geel
en alle zonnestralen komen heel
de stille lucht door als engelen.
Haar voetjes hangen te bengelen,
meisjesmondjes blazen gouden fluitjes,
gelipte mondjes lachen goudgeluidjes,
lachmuntjes kletteren op dit marmer,
ik zit en warm m'er.

Kijk ze nu loopen wendend om me heen,
't lijkt wel een herfst op de witte steen,
een herfst van dorre en geele kraakbladen,
engelen in wevegoudwaden,
zwevende guldvliezen,
neigende zonbiezen,
fluitende gouden zonnegeluiden,
ze leiden elkaar van uit het zuiden,
ze loopen over mijn marmersteen
in goudmuiltjes heen.
En 't lijkt of ze nu wel overal zijn,
de wereld is vol met een geelen goudwijn.

The sun. Yellow and gold is the world
and all the sun's rays are unfurled
through the silent sky, angel-sweet.
It dangles its little feet,
girls' mouths blow golden flutes,
from pursed lips gold laughter shoots,
on this marble the clatter of laughter's coins,
I sit and warm my loins.

Look at them walking turning around,
it's like autumn on the white stone ground,
autumn with leaves dry, crackly and yellow and yellow,
angels with robes gold-woven and mellow,
above, gold fleeces float away,
while sun rushes sway,
sunny gold whistling sounds from their mouth,
they guide each other up from the south,
across my marble floor they go
in golden slippers on tiptoe.
They seem to have flocked into every last space,
yellow gold wine fills this earthly place.

De stille weg
De maannachtlichte weg –

De boomen
De zoo stil oudgeworden boomen –
het water
het zachtbespannen tevreeë water.

En daar achter in 't ver de neergezonken hemel
met 't sterrengefemel.

The silent road
the glowing moonlit road –

the trees
the oh so still and aged trees –
the water
the gently tautened contented water,

And beyond, far off, the sunken sky
with the stars' wheedling cry.

De boomen waren stil,
de lucht was grijs,
de heuvelen zonder wil
lagen op vreemde wijs.

De mannen werkten wat
rondom in de aard,
als groeven ze een schat,
maar kalm en bedaard.

Over de aarde was
waarschijnlijk alles zoo,
de wereld en 't menschgewas
ze leven nauw.

Ik liep het aan te zien
bang en tevreden,
mijn voeten als goede lien
liepen beneden.

The trees were all still,
the sky was grey
the hills without will
lay in strange array.

The men were busy at toil
all about the place
as if digging treasure from soil,
though with measured pace.

Across the world's face
things were probably alike,
the world and the human race
are scarcely alive.

I walked and watched the scene
scared and content,
below, ever loyal and keen,
my footsteps bent.

De heide is maar stil,
het overal vol licht
en als een zilverspil,
het zonnelicht;

de wolken varen weg
over het vage blauwgrijze,
heel ver liggen witte weg
op zilvere wijze.

Ik voel den wind vergaan
om mijne ooren,
ik wilde wel vergaan
in 't licht te loore.

The heathlands quietly stand,
and all is full of light,
and like a silver strand
the sunshine all bright;

the clouds sail far away
across the vague grey-blue,
far off some white ones play
with a silver hue.

I feel the wind die down
about my ears;
I too would like to drown,
lost in light's spheres.

Het is weebleekerig grijs,
het regent wat,
de wind zingt een arme wijs,
de daken zijn nat.

Menschen gaan langzaam aan,
noemen het werken,
ernstig dagelijks gaan
zonder te merken.

O, om een lichte bleeke meid
die nu opbloeie,
wat weeïge lelieheid
mij, warme, moeie.

It's greyish-sickly-pale,
it's raining a bit
the wind sings a sorry tale,
the roofs are all wet.

People plod on their ways,
'earning their daily bread',
live out their earnest days,
do not turn their head.

Oh for a light pale girl to meet
with blossoming form,
some lilyness so sweet
for me, weary and warm.

Ik ben alleen in het lamplicht,
de dingen kijken met een glad gezicht,
om me in 't licht.

De dingen staan om me zoo stil
te luisteren wat de stilte wil,
vertellen wil.

En een verleden komt me aan de ooren
die stil opkijken en stil ophoren,
dingen verloren.

I'm alone in the lamplight,
impassive things absorb the sight,
round me in the light.

Things stand round me so still,
listening to silence's will,
what tales it will spill.

And a past now audibly nears
my quietly shocked and pricked-up ears,
things lost for years.

Gij staat zoo heel, heel stil
met uwe handen, ik wil
u zeggen een zoo lief wat,
maar 'k weet niet wat.

Uw schoudertjes zijn zoo mooi,
om u is lichtgedooi,
warm, warm, warm – stil omhangen
van warmte, ik doe verlangen.

Uw oogen zijn zoo blauw
als klaar water – ik wou
dat ik eens even u kon zijn,
maar 't kan niet, ik blijf van mijn.

En ik weet niet wat 't is wat
ik u zeggen wil – 't was toch wat.

You stand so very still
    with your hands, I've a will
to tell you sweet things, a lot,
but I don't know what.

Your shoulders are such a fine sight,
round you thawing of light,
warm, warm, warm – silently cloaked
in warmth, by desire I'm choked.

Your eyes are as blue
as clear water – I do
wish that I could be
you for a moment, but I stay me.

And what was it I wanted to say
to you?– it's flown away.

De lente komt van ver, ik hoor hem komen
en de boomen hooren, de hooge trilboomen,
en de hooge luchten, de hemelluchten,
de tintellichtluchten, de blauwenwitluchten,
trilluchten.

O ik hoor haar komen,
o ik voel haar komen,
en ik ben zoo bang
want dit is het sidderend verlang
wat nu gaat breken –
o de lente komt, ik hoor hem komen,
hoor de luchtgolven breken
rondom rondom mijn hoofd,
ik heb het wel altijd geloofd,
nu is hij gekomen.

Goud is het in de lucht als goude heiligen,
in labberlichtkleeden, de zeilige
die nu de aarde bevaren, bezeilen,
over de luchte meeren
met het zachtgladde kleed scheeren
en blijven wijlen
en komen keeren,
het zachte hoog luchtkleed tillende zeilen
ze heene en weer wiegelende
en blikken zich spiegelende
in de blauwe verwarmde watervlakken

O hoor je haar komen
met je zachte warme vingeren
hoog trillende in de bloeme-

The spring comes from afar, I hear it come hither
and the trees hear too, the tall trees that shiver,
and the tall skies, the heavenly skies,
the tingle-light skies, the blue-and-white skies,
shiver skies.

Oh I hear her come,
oh I feel her come
and I'm filled with fright
at trembling desires, all bright,
just about to break –
oh the spring comes, I hear it coming,
hear the sky waves break
around around my head
I always believed what they said
now it has come.

It is gold in the sky like golden saints' trails,
in baggy light robes, like sails
that now cross, sail the earth,
skim the lakes of air
with their soft smooth wear
and linger there
and come back again,
sails bearing the soft high cloak of air
to and fro swaying
and reflected looks playing
in the blue warmed water expanses.

Oh do you hear her come
with your soft warm fingers
trembling high in the flower

luchten die rondom klingelen?
met je vlottende hare
met het licht gebaren
van je blauwe vervlietende oogen
in het allerhooghooge
het hoogheilige luchtige goudluchtere licht?
hoor je 'm komen tederstil licht?

Laten we nu lachen
lachen lachen lachen
in zijn gezicht dat daar dagen
dagen doet in den dag,
laten we tranen weenen
weenen weenen weenen,
hij weent ook over ons henen
in zijn sneeuwglinsterdag.

Lentelicht is nu gekomen,
eindelijk is het gekomen,
o laten we toch lachen
lachen zoo licht als dagen,
want hij is er, hij is
en gij onz' droefenis
val toch in tintellichttranen
als bleeke vallende manen
stil in de lichternis.

skies that everywhere jangle?
with your hair floating bright
gesturing with the light
of your blue elusive eye
in the all high high
the high holy air gold lustrous light?
can you hear it coming, tender-still light?

Now let us laugh
laugh laugh laugh
in its face that is dawning
dawning there in the day,
tears let us weep
weep weep weep,
it weeps on us too
in its snow-sparkling day.

Spring light has now come,
at last it has come,
oh let us laugh then,
laugh as lightly as days,
for it's here, it's here
and you our sadness drear
fall in tingle tears light
like waning moons' pale light
still in the riot of light.

We voelen als twee
hooge, op stengel verhoogde lenterood-bloemen
midden in de lichtzee –
de lente is gekomen.

We feel like two
tall, spring-red flowers raised on stalks
amid the sea of light hue –
the spring has come.

Het strand was stil en bleek
ik zat doodstil en keek
naar de blauwe rimpeling –
er was ook windgezing.

Ik wist wie naast me zat
witrokkig en ze had
roosrood het glad gezicht –
er was ook veel zonlicht.

The beach was still and white
I sat still and relished the sight
of the blue rippling –
and I heard wind singing.

I knew who sat by me
with frock of white, and she
had a face smooth and rose-red –
the sun shone overhead.

Hè ik wou jij was de lucht
dat ik je ademen kon
en je zien in het hooge licht
en door je gaan kon.

Waar zijn je armen en je handen
en de witte overschoone landen
van je schouders en schijnende borst –
ik heb zoo'n honger en dorst.

Hey I wish you were the air
so I could breathe you in
and see you high in the light
and pass through your skin.

Where are your arms and your hands
and those white and wondrous lands
of your shoulders and shining breast –
by hunger and thirst I'm possessed.

Ik was toen een arme jongen
met te groot verlangen.

Lange luchten kwamen gevaren
Als lichte zeeëbaren
Over mijn hoofd, over mijn hoofd –
Mijn licht weenend hoofd.

Op rezen zonnen, vergingen
op hunne goudvurige zwingen,
moe viel mijn oog in mijn hoofd.

Mijn lichaam was toen zo wonderlijk,
elk lid afzonderlijk
leefde, ik zag het aan,
ik wist niet waar te gaan.

De lentenen kwamen met ademen,
sleepluchten in sleeplichte wademen
en lichte groene groenblondende schromen
licht lichtlijk straalvingerend om boomen
en glansplekkende wateren
en uitgestrekt klateren
des eeuwigen hemels
en ernstige kemels
van wolken, onderwijl loog over de lucht –
mijn jeugd, mijn jeugd, vlucht, vlucht,
vlucht niet te gauw voorbij,
maar blijf bij mij.

En donkere nachten
met purperblauw gedachten
en woorden uit omlage stad –
ik zat, ik zat
duisteromfonkeld, nachtoogbelonkeld,

I was a poor boy then
with too great a yen.

Long skies came sailing by
like the light sea waves fly
over my head, over my head –
my gently weeping head.

Up rose suns, and sank again
in their gold fiery train,
my eye sank tired in my head.

My body had a strange whim,
each individual limb
lived, I watched the show,
not knowing where to go.

And springs came in breathing air,
sky trails trailing white mists there
and scruples light green blonding
with trees light lightly brightly bonding
and waters sheen-stained
and glitter sustained
from the sky without end
where dour camels wend
made of clouds, while high above the skies
my youth, my youth, flies, flies,
don't fly past rapidly,
but stay with me.

Dark nights full of fears
with purple blue ideas
and words from below in the town –
I sat, I sat down,
stars darkly peering, night eyes peering,

omhoog tegen mijn kussen
gedchten te sussen
en wiegelen in mijn armen –
dat maakte zoo warme
mijn borst en adem langs mijn hals.

En dan de verlangenweeën
naar de schitterlichtzeeën,
naar het teervingrige spleen,
naar het ongehoord tintelgekwelen,
naar het strepend fellichtend ooglichtblauwen,
naar het lichtezwemen van vrouwen,
naar omtrekken licht die vallend kwijnen,
waar lichamen lijnen schijnen,
ver weg, ver weg –
terwijl hier ver weg
tranen neervallen, lachen opschijnen,
en 't leven in lichte treinen
lachend voorbijgaat alsof het leeft –
zie vèr, vèr geeft
zich de een na de ander op als golven,
golven, golven bedolven
de een na de ander, alles is lichten,
wit, wit verlichten
en scheem'rend schijnen
vlekken en lijnen ...
dat is de koninklijke dag

against the pillow I pushed,
my wild thoughts I shushed
and rocked them to and fro –
that made my chest so
warm and breath on my neck.

And then the pangs of desire
for the seas bright with fire
for tender fingery mooning,
for unheard-of tingling crooning,
for the striped glaring eyelight blue there,
for women's light-like air,
for a contour of light that falls and pines,
where bodies seem lines,
far away, far away –
while here far away
tears fall, smiles light up again
and life as in a lighted train
as if alive, smiles as it goes –
see far off those,
each of them like waves,
waves, waves, each of them caves
in one by one, all is a glow
white, white light show
and dusky shine
each blotch and line ...;
that is the royal day

dien een arm kind zag,
lang geleden, lang geleden,
verlangende, toch tevreden
niet wegdurvend uit verlangen,
lange, lange, lange.

En altijd weer dagen
goudzonspreidingvlagen
en mijn naakte armen omhoog in het licht
en mijn hoofd achterover naar 't licht,
en altijd wachten
wat in gedachten
geheel niet meer was dan wit licht.

a poor child saw one day,
ages ago, ages,
content though longing rages
the urge to stay was too strong,
long, long, long.

And again and again days
of gold spreading bursts of sun rays
and my naked arms aloft in the light
and head thrown back to the light,
always waiting to find
what in my mind
was nothing more than white light.

Stil zit ze, kijkt voor zich
langs hare wangen dood,
haar vingers bewegen zich
op hare beenen bloot.

Haar lichte haar is stil,
de oogen zijn niet te zien,
haar borsten staan stil,
niets te geschien.

Onder haar kin is rood –
warme schaduw,
en in de lichte schoot
donkerder schaduw.

She sits still, looks ahead
past her cheeks so red,
her fingers move everywhere
over her legs, both bare.

Her light hair is still,
the eyes cannot be seen,
her breasts too are still,
all is serene.

Beneath her chin red light –
warm shadow,
and in her lap, bright,
darker shadow.

'tIs zwart en donker.
kamerdonker als rook,
rood kolengeflonker,
daar boven holt de klok.

Langs de wanden bleekt flauw
een plaat en nog een –
het witte is lichtlauw
't lijkt alles lang geleên.

Hoor, het leven vliedt,
de klok holt, tik, tik –
zing het jammerlied
van het oogenblik.

It's black and dark,
chamber-dark as smoke,
red flicker of coal spark,
above, the racing clock.

Along the wall a pale, faint
picture and one more appears –
the white has a light lukewarm taint,
it all seems like bygone years.

Hear, life flies hell-bent,
the clock speeds tick, tick –
sing forth the lament
of the moment quick.

Het regende in de stad,
toen kwam er wat
muziek van straatmuzikanten,
die bliezen naar de kanten.

Toen voelde ik den leugen
van vroolijkheid in 't geheugen,
die men als kind eens heeft,
te dansen omdat men leeft.

The town was wet with the rain,
  then there came a strain
of music that buskers played,
blowing in a parade.

Then I felt the lie
of recalling joy gone by
that when young we sometimes feel,
so alive we dance a reel.

D e lucht was geel als geele chrysanthemen –
weien goudgroen in fonkelende atmosfeeren
van misten – goudgesmolten horizonnen –
door goudzongloedend miststrooigoud verduisterd.

Een gouden licht ter wereld gouden twijfel,
overal, overal, koninklijk twijfel,
twijfelend goud, gouden verwijfeling.

Troonden onz' harten in het gouden duister,
in 't goud onz' oogen als kristallen kronen.

The sky was yellow as yellow chrysanthemums –
  meadows of gold-green in sparkling atmospheres
of mists – molten gold horizons –
by gold sun glowing mist-strewn gold obscured.

A gold light abroad gold doubt.
everywhere, everywhere, royal doubt,
doubting gold, golden desperation.

Our hearts enthroned in the golden darkness,
in the gold our eyes like crystal crowns.

In de stilte van de stad
kwam ze, haar rok ruischte,
de witten handen had
ze stil, ik luisterde.

In the stillness of the town
she came, her dress swished,
her white hands lay down
quite still, I listened, hushed.

Toen bliezen de poortwachters op gouden horens,
buiten daar spartelde het licht op 't ijs,
toen vonkelden de hooge boometorens
blinkende sloeg de Oostewind de zeis.

Uw voeten schopten omhoog het witte sneeuwsel,
uw oogen brandden de blauwe hemellucht,
uw haren waren een goudgespannen weefsel,
uw zwierende handen een roôvogelvlucht.

De oogen in u die fonkenden jong-goude,
het bloed in u vloog wentel-roowiekend om,
de oogen der lucht die antwoordden zoo goude,
boven dreven ijsschuimwolken om.

IJskoud was het – lagen de waters bezijen
klinkklaar van ijs niet, spiegelend onder zon,
schreeuwde het hete licht niet bij 't overglijen,
omdat het snelvoetig de kou niet lijden kon.

De bolle blauwwangige lucht blies in zijn gouden
horenen omgespannen met zijn vuist –
de lucht kon 't wijs weerklinken niet meer houden,
berstte en brak en blauwe sneeuw vloog vergruisd.

De wereld was een blauwe en witte zale,
daar stond een sneeuw bed tintelsneeuw midde' in,

Then the gatekeepers' golden horns blared,
outside see the light on the ice writhe,
the tall tree towers sparkled and flared,
the East Wind swung its gleaming scythe.

Your feet kicked up the dusty white snow,
your eyes burned the blue sky's light,
your hair had a gold stretched tissue's glow,
your sweeping hands were eagles in flight.

The eyes in you sparkled young golden,
the blood in you swirled like incense about,
the eyes of the sky gave answers so golden,
above ice-foam clouds drifted about.

It was icy cold – the waters on each side
did not ring with ice, reflecting under sun,
the hot light did not scream as it seemed to slide,
since it could not bear cold, although it could run

The round, blue-cheeked sky blew into its gold
horns clutched firmly in its fist,
the wide echoing the sky could no longer hold,
and burst and broke and blue snow flew like grist.

The world was a chamber blue and white,
where a snow bed of tingling snow lay inbetween,

Uw goudhoofd naar zwaanveeren ging te dalen –
lachende laagt ge, over het veld, handblanke, blanktande, trantele
koningin.

your gold head descended to swan-down light –
laughing you lay, in the field, white-handed, white-toothed, playful
queen.

Het gouden zongezwier,
een oogenblik,
hoog maakt stil plezier
de leeuwerik.

De zon zwermt in goud goud,
fijn klinkt geklik
van schapebel – in 't goud
hoor leeuwerik.

De wolken gaan stil voort
op gouden grond,
ze zeggen zich geen woord
uit gouden mond.

The golden panache of the sun,
a moment, hark,
on high, still rapture of one
little lark.

The sun swarms in gold gold,
the fine clank, hark
of sheep's bell – in the gold
hear sound of lark.

The clouds scud past unheard
on golden ground,
they speak not one word,
from gold mouths no sound.

Ik wilde ik kon u iets geven
tot troost diep in uw leven,
maar ik heb woorden alleen,
namen, en dingen geen.

Maar o alzegenend licht,
witheerlijk, witgespreid licht,
daal op haar en laat haar nooit zijn
zonder uw zaligen schijn.

Zij is zoo stil en zoo zacht
als gij en niet onverwacht
zijt ge voor haar – zóó is
het water voor een zwemvisch.

Ik weet niet of zij u maakt
licht, als haar monde slaakt
adem, of dat zij door
u werd en dit u bevroor.

Zij is als de gouden zonmiddag,
een herfstige laatste biddag
van boomen en het graskruid
tot 't zonlicht, hoog boven ze uit.

Zij is het zilveren zwevende
het teere licht blozende gevende

I wish to you I could give
deep solace to help you live,
but words are all that I own,
nothing but names alone.

But, you beneficent light,
white splendid, white dispersed light,
descend on her and never let her go
without your blessed glow.

Still and soft like you she's made,
no surprise at you she's displayed –
she's in her own element,
as a fish for water is meant.

I know not if she makes
you light as her mouth takes
breath, or if she was made through
and materialised from you.

She's like the gold sun of late day,
a last autumn day to pray,
the grasses and all the trees,
to the sunlight, high up in the breeze.

She is the silvery drifting
the tender light-blushing gifting

licht, dat hemelhoog is,
goudeeuwig als 't herrefst is.

Haar oogen gaan wijd en zijd
boven mijn starend hoofd uit,
gouden en zilveren lichten
brengt ze op mensengezichten.

Ze weet haar licht niet, ze is
Zich zelve wel droefenis,
Ik wilde ik kon haar iets geven
Verlichtend het donkere leven.

light, high as the sky so tall,
gold eternal in the fall.

Her eyes roam far and wide
above my staring head,
gold and silver light traces
she puts on human faces.

She does not know her light,
feels to be sad is her plight,
I wish that I could give
her some light to help her live.

Zie ik hou van je,
ik vin je zoo lief en zoo licht –
je oogen zijn zoo vol licht,
ik hou van je, ik hou van je.

En je neus en je mond en je haar
en je oogen en je hals waar
je kraagje zit en je oor
met je haar er voor.

Zie je ik wou graag zijn
jou, maar het kan niet zijn,
het licht is om je, je bent
nu toch wat je eenmaal bent.

O ja, ik hou van je,
ik hou zoo vrees'lijk van je,
ik wou het heelemaal zeggen –
Maar ik kan het toch niet zeggen.

You see I love you, love,
   I think you're so sweet and so light –
your eyes are so full of light,
I love you, love. I love you, love.

And your nose and your mouth and your hair
and your eyes and your neck, where
your collar is and your ear,
your hair falling clear.

You see I'd like to be
you, but it's not to be,
the light is round you, you are
quite simply what you are.

Yes, I love you, love,
I love you so utterly,
I'd like to tell you in full –
But just *can't* tell you in full.

Al die grijze dagen
met hun stijve lachen
te leven en 't niet te meenen,
maar anders of anders gene.

En toch licht tevrede te zijn,
alleen wat oogenpijn
van 't fel geel lichten –
o, 's avonds de oogen te dichten!

De dagen zijn lichtreuzen
daar wandel ik laag tusschen.

All those grey days,
their stiff smirking malaise –
living them, insincere,
it must change or all disappear.

And yet being easy to please,
just pain in the eyes that won't ease
from the harsh yellow light –
oh, to close them at night!

The days are giants of light
lowly I wander among them.

Twee lampen schijnen,
    de spiegel schemerblauwt, er schrijnen
lichten in meubels rondom,
alle dingen zijn stom.

Ik hoor adem uit een vrouw
komen, ik wou
ik wou – ik zit zwaar en stil,
't is niets wat ik wil.

Hoor de klok rikketikken,
hij telt de oogenblikken.

Two lamps shining,
  the mirror dims and blues, whining
of lights in furniture around,
not a thing makes a sound.

I hear a woman's breath swish
as it comes, I wish
I wish – I sit heavy and still,
nothing enthuses my will.

Hear the clock tock tick,
it counts each moment's click.

De boomen golven op de heuvelen
boomhoofden stil in de nevelen
lentelichte zacht lentelicht.
De toren met zijn gezicht
daar midden in wijst deftig nog uren,
verbeel je uren, uren, uren –
't is om te stikken
in deze oogenblikken,
het kriebelend lachen
ik kan het haast niet verdragen,
ik stik
in dit krankzinnige lichte deftige oogenblik.

The trees wave on the hills
treetops in the mists still
spring-light spring light soft.
The tower's face aloft
in their midst still grandly shows hours,
imagine hours, hours, hours –
oh how they stifle
these moments that trifle,
the tickling laughter there
is more than I can bear,
I suffocate
under this mad light grand moment's weight.

SECONDARY READING

The edition used for these translations is *Herman Gorter. Verzen* (Amsterdam, 1977), edited with an introduction and notes by Enno Endt.

Two crucial secondary works are G. Stuiveling (ed.), *Acht over Gorter* (Amsterdam, 1978) and Enno Endt, *Herman Gorter documentatie 1864–1897* (Amsterdam, 1986). H. de Liagre Böhl's long-awaited biography, *Herman Gorter,* appeared in 1996.

BIBLIOGRAPHY OF GORTER'S POETRY
IN TRANSLATION*

Asakatura, S. & S., *Sekai meishishu*. Vol 15: *hokuo too* (Famous Poems of the World: Northern and Eastern Europe. Tokyo, 1960): [first canto of *Mei*]. *Japanese.*

Barnouw, A.J., *Coming After* (Piscataway, NJ, 1958). [opening lines of *Mei* (ll. 1–104); 'Mijn liefste was dood'.] *English.*

Bernáth, I. et al, *Németalföldi költök antológiája: Hollandok, Flamandok és Frízek* (Budapest, 1965). *Hungarian.*

Caraion, I. et al, *Antologie de poezie neerlandeza* (Bucharest, 1973). *Romanian.*

Carrasquer, F., *Antología de poetas holandeses contemporáneos* (Madrid, 1958). *Spanish.*

Carrasquer, F., *Antología de la poesía neerlandesa moderna* (Barcelona, 1971). *Spanish.*

Decroos, J., *Niederländische Gedichte aus neun Jahrhunderten* (Freiburg, 1960). *German.*

Dékány, K., *Holland költök Gortertöl Napjainkig* (Dutch Poets from Gorter to the Present. Budapest, 1986.) *Hungarian.*

Fagne, H. et al., *Anthologie de la poésie néerlandaise de 1850 à 1945* (Paris, 1975). *French.*

Gera, J., *A hétköznapi világ buvölete* (Budapest, 2000). *Hungarian.*

---

* This information derives mainly from the website of the Dutch Foundation for Literature: www.letterenfonds.nl

Greitemann, N., *Ein Strauss Narzissen* (Innsbruck, 1951). *German.*

Guarnieri, R et al., *Antologia delle letterature del Belgio e dell' Olanda* (Milan, 1970). *Italian.*

Hauser, O., *Die niederländische Lyrik von 1875–1900: eine Studie und Übersetzungen* (Grossenhain, 1901), *German.*

Havlíková, V et al., *V nizozemsku už nechci žit Czech* (Prague, 2007). *Czech.*

Holtzer, J. et al., *Nederlanda antologio: antologio de nederlanda poezio post la mezepoko en esperanto traduko* (Zaandam, 1987). *Esperanto.*

Kort, K. de et al., *Simbolismul European: vol I* (Bucharest, 1983). *Romanian.*

Malceva, N. et al., *Zapanoevropjskaya poeziya XX veka* (Moscow, 1977). *Russian.*

Muusses, M., *Landvinning: nutida Holländsk dikt i Svensk tolkning* (Stockholm, 1945). *Swedish.*

Prampolini, G., *La letteratura olandese e fiamminga (1880–1924)* (Rome, 1927), *Italian.*

Snell, A., *Flowers from a Foreign Garden: Selections from the Works of Modern Dutch Poets* (London, 1902) ['De lente komt van ver ...'] *English.*

Stuiveling, G., *A Sampling of Dutch Literature: Thirteen Excursions into the Works of Dutch Authors*. Translated and adapted by J. Brockway, (Hilversum, 1962). [16 lines from Barnouw's translation of *Mei*] *English.*

Vega, S., *Miwchar ha-sjira ha-holandit mi-1650 ad 1990* (s.l., 2000). *Hebrew.*

Venâncio, F., *Uma migalha na saia do universo: antologia da poesia neerlandesa do século vinte* (Lisbon, 1997). *Portuguese.*

Vitkovsky, E., *500 let poezii Niderlandov*, in *Konstantia* 1–6 (1995). *Russian.*

Weevers, T., *Poetry of the Netherlands in its European Context 1170–1930* (London, 1960). [26 ll. From *Mei* I, 99 ll. from *Mei* ii; 'Een roode roos is in mijn hand'; 'Zooals de maaiers 's avonds huiswaarts gaan ...'; 'De dag gaat open als een gouden roos ...] *English.*